U.S. ENVIRONMENTAL PROTECTION AGENCY
OFFICE OF INSPECTOR GENERAL

I0409999

Catalyst for Improving the Environment

Briefing Report

Steps Needed to Prevent Prior Control Weaknesses From Affecting New Acquisition System

Report No. 10-P-0160

June 28, 2010

Abbreviations

COOP	Continuity of Operations Plan
EAS	EPA Acquisition System
EPA	U.S. Environmental Protection Agency
FAR	Federal Acquisition Regulation
FIPS	Federal Information Processing Standards
ICMS	Integrated Contracts Management System
ITSC	Information Technology Service Center
NIST SP	National Institute of Standards and Technology, Special Publication
OAM	Office of Acquisition Management
OIG	Office of Inspector General
OMB	Office of Management and Budget

At a Glance

Catalyst for Improving the Environment

Why We Did This Review

We sought to determine to what extent the U.S. Environmental Protection Agency (EPA) took steps to prevent system control weaknesses in its current acquisition system from impacting the new replacement system. The Office of Inspector General contracted with Williams, Adley & Company, LLP, to conduct this review.

Background

The Integrated Contracts Management System (ICMS) supports the procurement needs of EPA offices. ICMS generates documents critical to the procurement process and recorded contract values totaling approximately $17.5 billion for Fiscal Year 2008. EPA is replacing ICMS with a new system called the EPA Acquisition System (EAS).

For further information, contact our Office of Congressional, Public Affairs and Management at (202) 566-2391.

To view the full report, click on the following link:
www.epa.gov/oig/reports/2010/20100628-10-P-0160.pdf

Steps Needed to Prevent Prior Control Weaknesses From Affecting New Acquisition System

What Williams, Adley & Company, LLP, Found

Stronger system controls over ICMS need to be addressed prior to transitioning to the new EAS. Williams, Adley & Company, LLP, noted that:

- System reporting does not always accurately associate a procurement action with the correct user who initiated the action.
- ICMS does not have an audit log to capture and allow monitoring of security events.
- No formal ICMS user training exists.
- The ICMS Continuity of Operations Plan and system backup procedures are not compliant with federal requirements.
- ICMS generates procurement documents in a format such that changes to the procurement documents can be made outside of the ICMS processing environment.

While it may not be practical for EPA to address these weaknesses within ICMS, EPA should take proactive steps to strengthen its system controls so these similar weaknesses do not exist in EAS.

What Williams, Adley & Company, LLP, Recommends

Williams, Adley & Company, LLP, recommends that the Director, Office of Acquisition Management:

- Modify EAS reporting to associate procurements with the correct user who initiated the action.
- Implement EAS security logging; develop and implement a formal process for storing, reviewing, and reporting violations recorded in security logs.
- Continue EAS Contracting Officer training and Getting Started training for EAS users prior to obtaining system access.
- Ensure the EAS contingency site is remote from the primary hosting site.
- Implement system controls, such as proper tracking and version control of procurement documents, to prevent a user from altering procurement documents outside of the EAS environment.

On June 9, 2010, we met with EPA officials to discuss this briefing. Appendix A contains EPA's response to the findings.

June 28, 2010

MEMORANDUM

SUBJECT: Steps Needed to Prevent Prior Control Weaknesses From Affecting
New Acquisition System
Report No. 10-P-0160

FROM: Rudolph M. Brevard *Rudolph M. Brevard*
Director, Information Resources Management Assessments
Office of Inspector General

TO: John R. Bashista, Director
Office of Acquisition Management
Office of Administration and Resources Management

Attached is the briefing report on the subject audit conducted by Williams, Adley
& Company, LLP (Williams Adley), on behalf of the Office of Inspector General
(OIG) of the U.S. Environmental Protection Agency (EPA). This report contains
findings that describe the problems Williams Adley identified and corrective
actions recommended. This report represents the conclusions of Williams Adley
and does not necessarily represent the final EPA position. Final determinations
on matters in this report will be made by EPA managers in accordance with
established audit resolution procedures.

The estimated cost for performing this audit, which includes contract costs and OIG
contract management oversight, is $199,174.

Action Required

In accordance with EPA Manual 2750, you are required to provide a written
response to this report within 90 calendar days. You should include a corrective
actions plan for agreed-upon actions, including milestone dates. We have no
objections to the further release of this report to the public. This report will be
available at http://www.epa.gov/oig.

If you or your staff have any questions regarding this report, please contact me at
(202) 566-0893 or brevard.rudy@epa.gov; or Harry Kaplan, Project Manager, at
(202) 566-0898 or kaplan.harry@epa.gov.

Attachment

Steps Needed To Prevent Prior Control Weaknesses From Affecting New Acquisition System

Results of Review

Audit Methodology

- Documented the information flows and system controls over the Integrated Contract Management System (ICMS).

- Identified five control weaknesses during the documentation phase.

- Issued audit findings and recommendations based on the control weaknesses identified during this review.

10-P-0160

Office of Acquisition Management (OAM) Datamart and Orbit Reporting Require Improvement

Finding 1

- OAM Datamart Reports do not always accurately associate a procurement action performed in ICMS with the correct ICMS user who initiated the action.

- OAM Datamart and Orbit Reports currently do not have the ability to display data below the Division level, which requires Service Center managers to manually manipulate reports to see data for their Service Center.

- Access to *ad-hoc* reporting capability within the OAM Datamart has not been granted to all Service Center managers.

10-P-0160

OIG Recommendations

Director, Office of Acquisition Management, should:

1-1 Modify the EPA Acquisition System (EAS) reporting to associate procurements with the correct user who initiated the action.

1-2 Modify EAS so the system creates reports at the individual Service Center level.

1-3 Grant Service Center managers access to EAS ad hoc reporting.

EPA's Response to the Finding

All three specific conditions will be remedied through implementing EAS which will include reporting that provides the correct Contracting Officer for an action, ability to report to the service center level, and a more user friendly *ad-hoc* reporting system for the customer base.

Audit log functionality needs improvement

Finding 2

ICMS does not have an audit log functionality to capture and monitor security events.

10-P-0160

OIG Recommendations

Director, Office of Acquisition Management, should:

2-1   Implement EAS security logging. Develop and implement a formal process for storing, reviewing, and reporting violations recorded in the security logs.

10-P-0160

EPA's Response to the Finding

OAM agrees with this condition, which will be remedied through implementing EAS. EAS provides auditing capabilities.

Formal ICMS User Training Program

Finding 3

Formal ICMS User Training was discontinued and replaced with a mentoring program in 2003 due to resource constraints.

10-P-0160

Formal ICMS User Training Program

- Contracting Officers will be required to take a 4-day training class to gain access to the EAS. All other users will have to complete the "Getting Started" module.

10-P-0160

OIG Recommendations

Director, Office of Acquisition Management, should:

3-1 Continue EAS Contractor Officer training and Getting Started training for remaining EAS users as a prerequisite for obtaining access to EAS.

3-2 Create and implement an EAS access policy requiring the EAS System Administrator to verify training attendance prior to granting a new user access to the application.

3-3 Retain documented evidence of each user's training attendance, through a sign-in sheet or other time-stamped means, to enforce compliance with the EAS access policy.

10-P-0160

EPA's Response to Finding

OAM will be providing full-system training to EAS customers. Users will not be provided access to EAS without having taken, at a minimum, the "Getting Started" module for requisitioners. Once EAS is deployed, it will be feasible to have Contracting Officer (CO) classes frequently enough to ensure the new COs are able to work efficiently as soon as they arrive. OAM will also be hosting webinars and user-group meetings to provide COs with refresher training and training on new functionality.

10-P-0160

ICMS Continuity of Operations Plan (COOP) and System Backup Procedures not in compliance with National Institute of Standards and Technology (NIST) guidance

Finding 4

- The ICMS production servers are hosted in Arlington, VA and the contingency site and tape storage facility in Washington, DC are geographically close in proximity.

- Aside from the servers at Potomac Yards, no backup servers exist for ICMS at the contingency site.

- No backup tapes existed for the Oracle database server that supports ICMS.

- OAM COOP has never been fully tested.

OIG Recommendations

Director, Office of Acquisition Management, should:

4-1 Implement an EAS contingency remote site separate from the primary hosting site.

4-2 Develop a mirror environment at EPA's Research Triangle Park (RTP) Campus in North Carolina or other designated site to assist the contingency facility in supporting system operations.

4-3 Test the EAS COOP after EAS implementation to verify compliance with federal and EPA guidance.

EPA's Response to Finding

- OAM's disaster recovery location in RTP, North Carolina, will remedy the close proximity of the production and contingency sites.

- OAM has had other disruptions with ICMS service and has been successful in bringing the system back up quickly and expediently. The single site is a critical risk component which OAM is mitigating through adding a mirrored disaster recovery site in RTP.

- OAM now has in place incremental backups as well as full tape backups for the oracle database server that supports the ICMS application.

10-P-0160

Draft and Final Contracts Version Control

Finding 5

- ICMS generates procurement documents in WordPerfect and stores them in PCDOCs, a document management system. These documents can then be saved by the users to their hard drive, thus allowing them to make changes to the procurement document outside of ICMS. The modifications, if done outside the system, will not be available in ICMS for management or reporting.

- Contract Specialists and Contract Officers may utilize various file types such as Microsoft Excel for procurement documents; however ICMS does not allow the upload of any file types other than WordPerfect and Lotus 1-2-3 for incorporation into a contract. PCDOCs can store any type of document.

OIG Recommendations

Director, Office of Acquisition Management, should:

5-1   Implement system controls, such as proper tracking and version control of procurement documents, to prevent users from altering procurement documents outside of the EAS environment.

5-2   Implement EAS functionality to upload various file types, such as Microsoft Word and Excel, to the system to ensure EAS is able to retain all documents associated with procurement.

10-P-0160

Status of Recommendations and Potential Monetary Benefits

		RECOMMENDATIONS				POTENTIAL MONETARY BENEFITS (in $000s)	
Rec. No.	Page No.	Subject	Status[1]	Action Official	Planned Completion Date	Claimed Amount	Agreed To Amount
1-1	4	Modify EAS reporting to associate procurements with the correct user who initiated the action.	O	Director, Office of Acquisition Management, Office of Administration and Resources Management			
1-2	4	Modify EAS so the system creates reports at the individual Service Center level.	O	Director, Office of Acquisition Management, Office of Administration and Resources Management			
1-3	4	Grant Service Center managers access to EAS ad hoc reporting.	O	Director, Office of Acquisition Management, Office of Administration and Resources Management			
2-1	7	Implement EAS security logging. Develop and implement a formal process for storing, reviewing, and reporting violations recorded in the security logs.	O	Director, Office of Acquisition Management, Office of Administration and Resources Management			
3-1	11	Continue EAS Contractor Officer training and Getting Started training for remaining EAS users as a prerequisite for obtaining access to EAS.	O	Director, Office of Acquisition Management, Office of Administration and Resources Management			
3-2	11	Create and implement an EAS access policy requiring the EAS System Administrator to verify training attendance prior to granting a new user access to the application.	O	Director, Office of Acquisition Management, Office of Administration and Resources Management			
3-3	11	Retain documented evidence of each user's training attendance, through a sign-in sheet or other time-stamped means, to enforce compliance with the EAS access policy.	O	Director, Office of Acquisition Management, Office of Administration and Resources Management			
4-1	14	Implement an EAS contingency remote site separate from the primary hosting site.	O	Director, Office of Acquisition Management, Office of Administration and Resources Management			
4-2	14	Develop a mirror environment at EPA's Research Triangle Park Campus in North Carolina or other designated site to assist the contingency facility in supporting system operations.	O	Director, Office of Acquisition Management, Office of Administration and Resources Management			
4-3	14	Test the EAS COOP after EAS implementation to verify compliance with federal and EPA guidance.	O	Director, Office of Acquisition Management, Office of Administration and Resources Management			

		RECOMMENDATIONS				POTENTIAL MONETARY BENEFITS (in $000s)	
Rec. No.	Page No.	Subject	Status[1]	Action Official	Planned Completion Date	Claimed Amount	Agreed To Amount
5-1	17	Implement system controls, such as proper tracking and version control of procurement documents, to prevent users from altering procurement documents outside of the EAS environment.	O	Director, Office of Acquisition Management, Office of Administration and Resources Management			
5-2	17	Implement EAS functionality to upload various file types, such as Microsoft Word and Excel, to the system to ensure EAS is able to retain all documents associated with procurement.	O	Director, Office of Acquisition Management, Office of Administration and Resources Management			

Agency Response

November 19, 2009

<u>**MEMORANDUM**</u>

SUBJECT: Response to Office of Inspector General (OIG) Finding Outline for Quality of Data in the U.S. Environmental Protection Agency's Integrated Contracts Management System (ICMS)

FROM: John C. Gherardini III, Acting Director
Office of Acquisition Management

TO: Rudolph M. Brevard, Director
Director, Information Resources Management Assessments
Office of Inspector General

We appreciate the opportunity to review and provide comments to this report.

Finding Number: 1 -   OAM Datamart and Orbit Reporting Improvements.

OAM agrees with specific condition 2.

In regards to condition 1, we would like to clarify that in our assessment, it is sometimes more important to know who signed the document (i.e. the Contracting Officer (CO)), and thus why we use MANAGEMENT ROLES so the Contract Specialist (CS) can generate and the CO can sign. Both the CS and CO are identified in MANAGEMENT ROLES. It is true that they are sometimes not updated which makes the data unreliable.

Also, the Access Control List would not be able to function in the manner identified for rectifying reporting issues. It is a function of the application that only identifies who is allowed to open and generate actions in ICMS on a contract and/or Task Order. It does not keep track of who initiated an action. Although not thru reporting, we are able to determine who initially generated an action (and everyone who subsequently accessed, edited, or printed the action) through DOCs History audit/tracking functionality.

OAM is in disagreement with specific condition 3, which states, "Many OAM Service Center Managers do not have access to run ad hoc reports from the OAM Datamart or Orbit". Although many OAM Service Center Managers do not have access to run ad hoc reports, it is only in the OAM data mart that this access has been limited. The complexity of the two systems (ICMS and SPEDI) and the numerous data fields made it very difficult for managers to create useable reports without help. We found it more appropriate to build reports for the managers and limit the ad-hoc reporting capability. Orbit, on the other hand, is not within OAM's control and our understanding is that anyone can gain access to ad-hoc reporting via a request to OCFO. We recommend changing the wording to "Access to ad hoc reporting capability within the OAM Data mart has not been granted to all Service Center Managers".

All three specific conditions will be remedied through the implementation of EAS which will include reporting that provides the correct Contracting Officer for an action, ability to report to the service center level and a more user friendly ad-hoc reporting system for the customer base.

Finding Number 2 – ICMS Audit Log Functionality Improvements

OAM is in agreement with Condition 1. Although we track and monitor access to our network infrastructure and the OAM environment as a whole and users are provided with specific IDs for ICMS and associated access, we do not have the capability to access inappropriate login attempts to ICMS specifically. Although users will not gain access, we are not able to identify those attempts to gain access to ICMS. However, this condition will be remedied via EAS as the software does provide auditing capabilities.

Finding Number 3 – Formal ICMS User Training Program

OAM is in agreement that the ICMS training was replaced with mentoring due to resource constraints. In regards to EAS, we will be providing EAS training to EAS customers. This training is not "upgrade" training but full system training. Although the training is not mandatory, users will not be provided access to EAS without having taken, at a minimum, the "Getting Started" module for requisitioners. Contracting Officers (CO) will have to take the 4 day class to gain access. Once EAS is deployed, it will be feasible to have Contracting Officer classes frequently enough to ensure the CO is able to work efficiently as soon as they arrive. In those cases where a class is not scheduled for the day a CO is scheduled to take the class, their manager will need to assign them a mentor and it will be required that the Contracting Officer attend the next available class. We will also be providing webinars and having user-group meetings to provide Contracting Officers with refresher training and training on new functionality.

In addition, we feel that there may be some confusion between data migration trial training and the EAS training itself. The EAS data migration trial training does concentrate on the reviewing of data coming into the EAS system from ICMS. The EAS training itself will deal with the functionality of EAS to include the creation of new contracts, importance of clean data by using drop down lists, etc. They are two separate training classes.

Finding Number 4 – ICMS Continuity of Operations Plan (COOP) and System Backup Procedures are not compliant with National Institute of Standards and Technology (NIST) Guidance

OAM is in agreement with specific condition 1, which states, "The ICMS production servers are hosted in Arlington, VA and the contingency site and tape storage facility in Washington, DC are geographically close in proximity." This will be remedied with the implementation of our disaster recovery site in RTP, North Carolina.

In regards to specific condition 2, which states, "Aside from the servers at Potomac Yards, no backup servers exist for ICMS at the contingency site." We would like to suggest the wording be clarified to read:

- No backup servers exist for ICMS aside from the servers in Potomac Yards. Should a continuity event render Potomac Yards unavailable, OAM would not have equipment available to restore ICMS to service.

In regards to the specific instances identified under condition 3, which states, "No backup tapes existed for the Oracle database server that supports the ICMS." When the audit began, this was a correct finding but has since been remedied. We now have in place incremental backups as well as full tape backups for the oracle database server that supports the ICMS application.

In regards to specific condition 4, which states, "4) The Office of Acquisition Management (OAM) COOP has never been fully tested." We would like to suggest the wording be clarified to read:

- The Office of Acquisition Management (OAM) COOP, which addresses the scenario of a continuity event rendering Potomac Yards unavailable, has never been fully tested.

We have had other disruptions with ICMS service and have been successful in bringing the system back up quickly and expediently. The virtualized environment that we have in place, in conjunction with RAID level 5 technologies, allows us to quickly respond to problems in the infrastructure. The single site is a critical risk component which we are mitigating thru the addition of a mirrored disaster recovery site in RTP.

Finding Number 5 – Draft and final contracts version control issues

OAM agrees to the specific conditions in general but feel they are inaccurate as stated. The application, PCDOCs, is a storage utility for documents and is misrepresented as functionality only used by ICMS. Below is a more accurate re-statement of the issues.

- ICMS generates procurement documents in WordPerfect and stores them in PCDOCs, a document management system. These documents can then be saved by the users to their hard drive, thus allowing them to make changes to the procurement document outside of

22

ICMS. The modifications, if done outside the system, will not be available in ICMS for management or reporting.

- Contract Specialists and Contract Officers may utilize various file types such as Microsoft Excel for procurement documents; however ICMS does not allow the upload of any file types other than WordPerfect and Lotus 1-2-3 for incorporation into a contract. PCDOCs can store any type of document.

Also in reference to the status information, please note that EAS will have all active contract documents verified during deployment but not **closed** contracts. Inactive contracts would still be verified as they are needed for actions in the future but it may be after a Contracting Office deploys.

Distribution

Office of the Administrator
Assistant Administrator, Office of Administration and Resources Management
Agency Follow-up Official (the CFO)
Agency Follow-up Coordinator
Director, Office of Acquisition Management, Office of Administration and
       Resources Management
General Counsel
Associate Administrator for Congressional and Intergovernmental Affairs
Associate Administrator for Public Affairs
Audit Follow-up Coordinator, Office of Administration and Resources Management
Audit Follow-up Coordinator, Office of Acquisition Management,
       Office of Administration and Resources Management
Inspector General

www.ingramcontent.com/pod-product-compliance
Lightning Source LLC
Chambersburg PA
CBHW081810280526
45789CB00008B/3082